LITTLE INSTRUCTION
BOOK OF
THE RICH & FAMOUS

548 Helpful Hints for Living
a Prosperous and Happy Life
from 108 Celebrities

by ROBERT J. LAWN

CCC PUBLICATIONS

Published by

CCC Publications
1111 Rancho Conejo Blvd.
Suites 411 & 412
Newbury Park, CA 91320

Manufactured in the United States of America

Cover © 1995 CCC Publications

Cover/Interior production by Oasis Graphics

ISBN: 0-918259-96-7

If your local U.S. bookstore is out of stock, copies of this book may be obtained by mailing check or money order for $5.99 per book (plus $2.50 to cover postage and handling) to: CCC Publications, 1111 Rancho Conejo Blvd., Suites 411 & 412, Newbury Park, CA 91320

Pre-publication Edition - 10/95

*Everyone knows how to live a useful
and productive life.*

But how can you become Rich and Famous?

*The best way is to learn from the people
who have done just that!*

Yes, The Rich and Famous. From what other
source can we learn so much? They're the ultimate

set of achievers, go-getters, winners, and do-ers in our society. They have lived lives most of us only dream about. From movie idols to sports stars, from glamorous models to captains of industry, this select group is truly remarkable. And yet, with all their fame and fortune, they have to live the same twenty-four hours each day that we do. That's where this book comes in.

"Little Instruction Book of The Rich & Famous" reflects the humorous everyday lessons that life has taught our "Rich and Famous" friends. And while this book may not bring you riches or fame, it promises to give you more than your money's worth in laughs.

To my beautiful wife Kim,
without whose hard work and sacrifice
this book couldn't have happened.

———— ◆ ————

Richard Simmons

- It's impolite to call an overweight supermarket cashier a "chubby checker."

- Never trade a fat philosopher food for thought.

- Ironically, the smaller your love handles are, the more likely they'll be held.

- No matter how much he insists, never refer to a gay aerobic instructor as "The Thigh Master."

2

Bill Clinton

- ◆ Always steer your raft away from the whitewater.

- ◆ Never try to fit a square Vice-President into an Oval office.

- ◆ Always be sure to salute The Commander-in-Chief ...and her husband, too.

- ◆ One good term deserves another.

- Keep your eyes on your fries.

- Anyone who tells you they didn't inhale is full of hot air.

- Removing important documents from a crime scene can *Foster* a sense of distrust.

- Sometimes it only takes one jack-ass to bring down an entire party.

3

The Dream Team:

Johnny Cochran, Robert Shapiro, F. Lee Bailey et al.

- Hiring the best attorney that money can buy will ensure that the only thing hung is the jury.

- Never chase an ambulance with it's reverse lights on.

- A lawyer who forgets his briefs only leaves his client exposed.

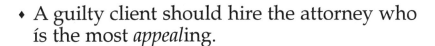

- A guilty client should hire the attorney who is the most *appeal*ing.

- A good friend will always help an alcoholic pass the bar.

- Never let little things like the truth stand in the way of a good payday.

4

Cindy Crawford

- A picture is worth a thousand bucks.

- Don't expect a girl who eats no fat to smile when she says "cheese."

- Walking through a construction site at lunchtime will make even the homeliest girl feel feel like a supermodel.

- Never buy a swimsuit you can't fit into your change purse.

- You can pose a difficult question, but never question a difficult pose.

- Never send a dog down a catwalk.

5

Ice Cream Kings
Ben & Jerry

- If you expect life to be all Peaches and Cream, you're headed down a Rocky Road.

- Never call a homosexual ice cream vendor a "Dairy Queen."

- Never let a hungry reporter near your scoop.

- Don't expect your lactose-intolerant dinner host to join you in a bowl of ice-cream. Some people can dish it out but they can't taste it.

- No matter how many exciting options you give them, some people just have a plain vanilla personality.

6

Jay Leno

- Always try to keep your chin up no matter how big it is.

- Never hire a sidekick who is only interested in blowing his own horn.

- Unless you want to participate in a late night war, don't come home to your wife smelling of cheap perfume.

- Go to the Post Office if you feel the need to see a Letter man.

Senator Robert Packwood

+ No matter how much trash is in *yours,* never grab your secretary's *can.*

+ An equal opportunity employer should be willing to harass women of all ethnic backgrounds.

+ Never criticize a politician for a mere slip of the tongue.

+ Never ask your secretary to sit on your lap and talk about whatever pops up.

8

Dr. Joyce Brothers

- ◆ Never send a stressed-out comedian to the Funny Farm.

- ◆ Don't jump to conclusions when a toy-store owner tells you that he's lost his marbles.

- ◆ Never give a manic depressive a mood ring.

- ◆ Never sing Christmas Carols to someone who is *Claus*trophobic.

- Don't accuse an unemployed cartoonist of having Peanuts envy.

- Never trust a schizophrenic who talks behind his own back.

- Lying on the couch all day is the reason why most people are depressed in the first place.

9

Sharon Stone

- You'll definitely improve your movie career if you're willing to uncross your legs on cue.

- Even if you live in a glass house, don't hesitate to cast a Stone

- Never refer to someone who makes $4 million per picture as "a dumb blond."

10

Gloria Estefan

• If you use the calendar as your primary method of birth control, most likely, *the rhythm is gonna get ya.*

• Don't enter the recording business unless you're prepared for back-breaking amounts of work.

• Hearing a steamy bilingual ballad is enough to make any man want to sample a foreign tongue.

11

Dr. Jack Kevorkian

- Don't sneak up on people. You could scare them to death.

- Never kick another man's bucket.

- Where there's a notarized will, there's a way.

- Don't wait until the last minute to see your doctor.

- Don't tell a friend they look good in an outfit you wouldn't be caught dead in.

- Never offer treatment to a mathemetician who says his days are numbered.

Heidi Fleiss

◆ Never kiss and tell unless subpoenaed.

◆ Have an answering service. You could miss a lot of important calls while you're tied up with a client.

◆ If you care for your black book properly, it will keep its *Sheen*.

◆ Always be willing to bend over backwards for your customers.

- Early to bed with whips, chains and ties, makes a girl healthy, wealthy and wise.

- Never trust a magician who wants to see your book of tricks.

13

Mike Tyson

- Always be wary of a *knockout* babe.

- Don't feel boxed in by a career choice. Do what you love.

- Remember, boxing is like recess. You can't start swinging 'til you hear the bell.

- Don't treat your spouse like a punching bag. She may decide to throw in the towel.

- If you're not careful on New Year's Eve, you could end up *punch*-drunk.

- Never *hit on* someone until you count to ten.

14

Danielle Steele

◆ Spontaneous gifts from time to time will keep any *romance novel*.

◆ No marriage has ever ended because a husband found his wife curled up in bed with a good book.

◆ Sometimes you need to be willing to turn the page and start a new chapter in your life.

◆ Men should be like a cup of coffee: tall, dark, and strong enough to keep you up all night.

15

Denzel Washington

◆ If you spend too much time at the zoo watching the giraffe, you'll find your time with *The Pelican Brief.*

◆ Tell your kids it's not nice to refer to a strict nun as a *Devil in a Blue Dress.*

◆ A good equation for a successful movie career is "When asked to be X, don't ask "y?"

◆ You better have seven of *George* Washington's pictures to fork over if you hope to see one of Denzel's.

16

Robin Leach

⋄ If you have rich and famous friends, try not to be a *Leach*.

⋄ No matter how wealthy you are, bathe every day. Nobody likes a person who is *filthy* rich.

⋄ Don't be selfish. Let the butler borrow one of the yachts for the weekend.

- If you try to live as a jet-setter, you may be grounded by debt.

- Never ask an alcoholic fisherman about his champagne wishes and caviar dreams.

Japanese Prime Minister *Horahuchi*

• Some guests who neglect to remove their shoes when they enter your home are actually doing you a favor.

• A president shouldn't start a trade war unless his citizens are prepared to say "sayanara" to high-quality luxury automobiles.

• If you have too many kamikazis, you could end up getting bombed.

• A true economic power doesn't need a military arsenal because the *yen* is mightier than the sword.

18

Weight Loss Expert
Jenny Craig

- Losing twenty pounds before a job interview can tip the scales in your favor.

- The first secret to losing weight is to stop biting off more than you can chew.

- There's only *one* way to quickly lose one-hundred pounds: visit a casino in England.

- If a girl can control her appetite, she'll find it much easier to whet a man's.

19

Wilt Chamberlain

- Never pass on a 3-on-1.
- A single's bar is the best place to play a *pick-up* game.
- Ironically, the better you are at making a *pass*, the more you'll *score*.
- If you compliment a cheerleader, you stand a better chance of seeing her pom-poms in action.

- When you hear a tall-tale, always consider the source.
- Some men's imaginations never *Wilt* no matter how long it's been since they've gotten lucky.

20

Mel Gibson

- Never refer to a small ham omelette as a *Hamlet*.

- Don't stand too close to a smoker. Their breath can be a *Lethal Weapon*.

- A *Tequila Sunrise* is usually followed by a Tylenol sunset.

- Don't hike up another man's kilt unless you've got a *Braveheart*.

21

Boy George

- Don't discriminate against an employee on the basis of gender, or lack thereof.

- A man doesn't *always* have to wear the pants in his family.

- If the fuchsia pump fits, wear it.

- Never try to build a toolshed while your nails are drying.

Oprah Winfrey

- The best way to become a wealthy talk-show host is to put your money where your mouth is.

- Try not to judge people based on their race, creed, color, sexual preference, number of body parts pierced, whether or not they've been abducted by aliens, or if they were someone else in a previous life.

♦ Never interview a cannibal. They'll try to talk your ear off.

♦ Never say in five minutes what you could have stretched to sixty.

Judge Lance Ito

- Making America watch the entire O.J. trial was cruel and unusual punishment.

- Don't be afraid to give a convicted murderer *the Juice.*

- Never judge a man until you've walked a mile-long trail left by his bloody shoes.

- The best way to make your point to criminals is to use really long *sentences.*

- Drink a variety of breakfast beverages. O.J. every day is enough to make anyone puke.

- Never sit downwind from a defense attorney.

24

Colin Powell

♦ Never vote for a candidate who will only tell you his name, rank, and serial number.

♦ An upset Colin usually leads to serious G.I. problems.

♦ Make sure you support a soldier during his *book-tour*-of-duty.

- A soldier who's been stuck in a foxhole for a week will always out*rank* you.

- Vote for a candidate who can campaign more before 9 A.M. than most politicians do all day.

25

Mario Andretti

+ Just because you're going in circles doesn't mean you're not getting anywhere.

+ No matter how good you are in bed, women generally don't appreciate a victory lap.

+ *Nobody* likes a backseat driver.

+ If your mechanic is deaf, *you* have to make sure that the squeaky wheel gets the grease.

- The fastest way from Sweden to Denmark is to cross the Finnish line.

- Never ask a transvestite race-car driver if he wants to go drag.

26

Jesse Jackson

◆ Getting off your lazy ass to apply for a job really shows Affirmative Action.

◆ If you're going to judge someone by the color of their skin, make sure it's during a suntanning contest.

◆ You'll ruin your opthamologist's day if you tell him you hope for a color-blind society.

27

Whoopi Goldberg

• If you're afraid to audition for a challenging role, you won't stand a *Ghost* of a chance.

• Don't judge a black woman's theatrical ability until you've at least seen the *Sister Act*.

• Passing gas in the middle of your stand-up routine makes for great *Comic Relief.*

28

Mary Kay

- Never argue with a cosmetic saleswoman unless you're prepared to *make-up* afterwards.

- Discussing your sex-life in public is a great way to make a grown man blush.

- *Astringent* workout will always make you *toner*.

- Don't come home with lipstick on your collar unless you're prepared to kiss your marriage good-bye.

- It's not polite to ask a woman why she doesn't take her make-up when she goes to powder her nose.

Arnold Shwarzenegger

- No one likes to be a *Terminator*, but sometimes it's necessary to fire an unproductive employee.

- Don't let a German accent stop you from living the American dream.

- Be careful when taking a date to the movies. You may only seek *action and adventure*, while she's interested in *romance*.

- You can exercise your body with dumbells, but to exercise your mind you need to be around smart people.

- When your muscles are bulging but your testicles are disappearing, it may be time to cut back on your steroids.

Newt Gingrich

+ Turning up the volume of your *speaker* may improve your *party's* popularity.

+ Out with the old, in with the Newt.

+ Vote for term limits. The House is not meant to be a home.

+ If your Mom airs your dirty laundry on national TV, you'll be *Chung*-out-to-dry.

- In America, if you want a contract to be taken seriously, you need to put it in writing.

- Never vote for a useless *Bill*.

31

David Letterman

- Too much coffee during the day can make for a *Late Nite*.

- Don't spend your life trying to get on someone else's Top 10 List.

- Sometimes it really pays to be stuck behind a desk all day.

- Pulling the chair out from under someone as they're trying to sit down is really a Stupid Human Trick.

- Sometimes your *station* in life needs to change.
- Don't let a bad hair day affect your sense of humor.

32

Bruce Lee

- The problem with kicking the crap out of twenty Chinese guys is that an hour later you feel like fighting again.

- The only ones who need their hands registered as dangerous weapons are teenage boys.

- The best philosophy for a karate match is to chop 'til you drop.

• He who dunk his cookie too quickly end up finding fortune in tea leaves.

• Learn how to use your hands to defend yourself. Don't take karate lessons just for kicks.

33

Vidal Sassoon

- The best stylists are good listeners. No one wants to hear someone blowing hot air all day.

- Never hire a shampoo girl who thinks she's *head and shoulders* above her co-workers.

- Too much *teasing* can make it difficult for a girl to let her hair down.

- If you highlight someone's hair who has a bad case of dandruff, you could end up with frosted flakes.

- Don't request a permanent unless you're prepared for a hair-raising experience.

34

Mayor Marion Barry

+ Never expect a crooked man to keep to the straight and narrow.

+ Never dip your straw in another man's *coke*.

+ Voting for a crackpot may cause your city's progress to be *arrested*.

+ Keep your nose clean.

+ It's not a good idea to expect a drug-addict to take your city to new highs.

Dolly Parton

- Never argue with an emotional plastic surgeon. They tend to make mountains out of molehills.

- Don't call two owls a pair of hooters.

- Sometimes a boob-job is the only way to keep your career from going *bust*.

- To be a successful singer, stay *abreast* of musical trends.

36

Joe Montana

+ Run a lot of "shotgun" plays if your center ate baked beans the night before.

+ Before cooking pork, always remove the "pigskin."

+ It is better to kick than to receive.

+ Never call someone a "tight-end" unless you're playing football.

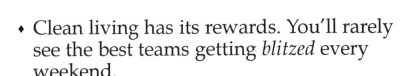

- Clean living has its rewards. You'll rarely see the best teams getting *blitzed* every weekend.

- Don't dress like a dork to go out to a singles bar. You'll end up making a lot of *incomplete* passes.

37

Mother Theresa

◆ Always be willing to change a *filthy habit*.

◆ If you give an anonymous donation to the poor, it'll be a blessing in disguise.

◆ Don't look a gift cow in the mouth.

◆ Always treat your mother like the saint she is.

The Menendez Brothers

- Think twice before you withhold your kid's allowance.
- No matter how much you like to shoot off *your* mouth, never shoot off your parents'.
- A spoiled *pair* eventually turns rotten.
- Never take your parents *out* for target practice.
- Never shoot the hand that feeds you.

39

Ross Perot

- It's best to vote for someone you think is just like you, give or take a billion dollars.

- When someone else is speaking, be all ears.

- Be spontaneous. Starting a *party* can be fun.

- Take care of personal problems before you run for office. You can't be elected President if voters see a terrible *Vice.*

- Even a short politician can be elevated into the limelight if he stands on an honest *platform.*

40

Hulk Hogan

◆ Never atomic-kick a man when he is down.

◆ If you do something you know is wrong, be prepared to wrestle with your conscience.

◆ The best parents use a tag-team approach to deal with their kid's antics.

◆ You'll never have a successful relationship if you *throw in the towel* every time you're *on the ropes*.

41

Hugh Grant

- Always buy a car with a tilt-steering wheel.

- No matter how much you like to drive, never take your *rod* out on the boulevard.

- Never haggle with a pro.

- Always buckle up no matter how *Divine* you think the ride will be.

- If you pay to put your hands all over a woman, don't be surprised if you end up being asked for your fingerprints.

- No matter how badly your money is burning a hole in your pocket, never whip it out in public.

42

John Madden

+ A great way to handle an unruly child is a well-placed *time-out*.

+ Never probe an irritated jock.

+ Sometimes the best decisions are made by a flip of the coin.

+ If you spend all day Sunday in front of the television, you'll surely *Madden* your wife.

- A healthy diet will reduce the chances of a *sudden death*.

- Ask the dentist for extra gas if you get too nervous during his *two-minute drill*.

- Watching too much football can make it difficult to *tackle* those household chores.

43

Nike Chairman
Philip Knight

+ Don't buy expensive sneakers and expect your parents to *foot* the bill.

+ Never judge a man 'til you've walked a mile in his Air Cross-Trainers™.

+ Just because you're pregnant doesn't mean you have to be barefoot.

- When your parents tell you to do your homework, don't argue, *Just Do It!*

- If the shoe fits, buy it!

- Don't waste your money on overpriced sneakers if you're on a shoestring budget.

Jerry Seinfeld

- Laughter is the best medicine for someone with a broken funny bone.

- He who laughs last didn't get the joke.

- Show up early on New Year's Eve or you'll find yourself at the back of the *punchline*.

- Don't waste your time telling a knock-knock joke to a doorbell salesman.

- Don't treat a friend to a comedy show unless you don't mind them having a laugh at your expense.

45

Jack Nicklaus

- Even if you're playing the Irish Open, never take a *Mulligan*.

- Spending too much time with your golf clubs can drive a *wedge* into your marriage.

- Never cry "fore" in jest.

- A few tough times in life are par for the course.

- A farmer who likes to golf better know his ass from a hole in the ground.

Julia Child

- Spoiled broth can come from even one-cook kitchens.

- Cooking is a great way to use up your spare *thyme*.

- Don't put a relationship on the backburner unless you're prepared for it to cool off.

- Going bottomless on a sunny day could make your *rump roast*.

- If you refuse a Christmas dinner invitation, you could end up cooking your own goose.

- A real man not only brings home the bacon, he makes it sizzle as well.

47

Ted Kennedy

- Never take a long drive off a short pier.
- Opening the car door for your date can make the evening a swimming success.
- Don't run for President on a "two kegs in every garage" platform.
- Running against an anal-retentive conservative can be a real cam*paign-in-the-ass*.

Princess Diana

- The best way to get back at an unfaithful prince is to grab his *family jewels*.

- Don't open the door on your spouse while he's on the *throne* until after you've heard the *Royal flush*.

- When your Prince tells you he's going on a *fox*hunt, make sure he takes his dogs with him.

- Watching your Prince turn into a toad is enough to make a *Lady Di*.

49

Calvin Klein

+ In business, it's never fashionable to be late.

+ For some people, good looks are in the *jeans.*

+ To make it in the fashion industry, you need to be both open to new ideas and *clothes*-minded.

◆ Sometimes the *man* makes the clothes.

◆ Remember: rich people are no different than you. They still put on their three-thousand dollar cashmere Italian-cut pants one leg at a time.

Stephen King

+ Driving with a teenager can be a terrifying experience.

+ Don't visit your girlfriend too early in the morning. How some women look without their make-up is frightening.

+ Always check the babysitter's bedtime story selections.

- Don't always assume your children are fibbing when they tell you there is a monster under their bed.

- Showing someone the amount of taxes taken from their weekly paycheck is the best way to get a blood-curdling scream.

51

Tom Cruise

- Dancing around in your underwear with the drapes open is *Risky Business*.

- Acting is hard work. Don't expect to just *Cruise* your way to the top.

- Target-shooting should be done in fair weather. Never shoot your *Top Gun* in the *Rain, Man*.

52

Kenny G.

- It's perfectly acceptable to blow your own horn.

- Don't walk through a dark music store — you may slide on a trombone.

- Never lend your reed to a garlic-lover.

- Always clean your *instrument* thoroughly after each use.

- Don't assume someone is always horny just because they like a little sax now and then.

53

Cal Ripken, Jr.

- No matter how badly you're itching to play, don't scratch your crotch on national TV.

- Never try to get to second base on a first date.

- When dealing with salesmen, never go for the first pitch.

- If you don't take the *world serious*, you'll end up having a ball.

• Don't expect to be called up from the farm team if you can't hit the broad side of a barn.

• You don't necessarily have to have a magnetic personality to be an "Ironman."

54

Bill Gates of Microsoft Inc.

• If you don't stand up straight, you could get a *floppy* disk.

• Never hesitate to go *Windows* shopping.

• Don't be afraid of a *mouse* in the house.

• Traveling the entire Information Superhighway without stopping can be a hard drive.

- Don't compute your chickens till they've hatched.

- If you catch someone holding your laptop over a tea kettle, they're probably trying to steam open your E-mail.

- Never ask a senior citizen how much memory they have.

55

Tim Allen

- The skin between your underwear and your toolbelt should *never* see the light of day.

- Don't try to be a *handy*man if you're all thumbs.

- Always keep three hammers on hand: one for the morning, one for the evening, and one for all over this land.

- Remember, with $50,000 worth of tools, anybody could fix up This Old House.

- As far as inventions go, the hammer hits the nail right on the head.

- The best way to succeed as a comedian is to grunt softly, but carry a big shtick.

56

Joey Buttafuoco

- Always ask your date for age verification.

- If a teenager comes into your garage showing her *pink slip*, feel free to give her a tune-up.

- Cheating on your spouse can *trigger* marital difficulties.

• Don't expect to be forgiven if you choose to be unfaithful. It's not like someone held a gun to your head.

• Be wary if someone tells you they are fatally attracted to you.

57

Snoop Doggy Dog

+ You're not done recording 'til the producer says it's a *rap*.

+ If you mess around with the law, you're barking up the wrong tree.

+ Don't forget your wedding anniversary unless you want to end up in the doghouse.

+ Anti-white prejudice is wrong. The Man is Snoop Doggy Dog's best friend.

- Never buy a rap record that sounds like Doggy-dogcrap.

- You can take the boy out of the 'hood, but you can't take the hood' out of the boy.

58

Elvis Presley

• Visit Alcatraz, it's quite a Jailhouse Rock.

• Saying your prayers before dinner will make any home a *Grace*land.

• Always buy an office chair that allows you to swivel your hips.

- When his little princess married a freak, you can bet that the "King" is turning over in his grave.

- A bad real estate investment could leave you with a *Heartbreak Hotel*.

59

Saddam Hussein

+ Thou shalt not covet thy neighbor's oil.

+ Never draw a line in the sand unless you're prepared to back it up.

+ Let everyone in the family choose the weekend activities. Don't be a dictator.

+ Only bullies kick desert sand in a smaller country's face.

+ Keep a bottle of Lysol on hand. It'll help you fight germ-warfare around the house.

60

Billy Graham

- Never change your prepared sermon at the last moment. Preach what you practice.

- Success is a *Testament* to hard work.

- Don't start reading the Bible unless you have a lot of free time. A *Good Book* is hard to put down.

- For God's sake, don't take everything you hear as *Gospel*.

- He that farteth in Church shall sit in his own pew.

61

Howard Stern

- Dropping a hairdryer in your wet swim trunks could give you a *shockjock*.

- If you don't know what station your clock radio is tuned to, you may be in for a rude awakening.

- Respect the first amendment, or you may be left speechless.

• Give a *Stern* reprimand to your kids if they use language from on-air radio personalities.

• Listen to F.M. in the A.M. for all your S & M needs.

David Copperfield

- Watch out for rabbit turds in your magic hat.

- Never wear a white straightjacket after Labor Day.

- It's magical how many old friends reappear after you make a lot of money.

- A guy who offers to give you the shirt off his back probably has something up his sleeve.

- Never dip your wand in company ink. It could be a bad move to break it off with the girl who saws you in half every night.

Andre Agassi

• To be an outspoken tennis star you often have to raise a *racquet*.

• Don't expect all European tennis fans to act alike. You may find the Germans reserved and *The French Open*.

• Treat sex as a serious commitment. Ideally, the perfect match should start from *love* before any scoring begins.

- Having a big ego can be a plus. It takes a plenty of *balls* to become a professional tennis player.

- You're wasting your time playing tennis with a politician. Most of them don't know how to *serve*.

Alex Trebek

- No one likes a know-it-all.

- The only stupid question is the one that goes unasked.

- A tactful way to disagree with your boss is to phrase your answers in the form of a question.

• Unfortunately, when dealing with the I.R.S., the wrong answer can put your earnings in *Jeopardy*.

• Trick-or-treaters should never hit the buzzer until they know the right question.

65

Chairman of The Federal Reserve Bank
Alan Greenspan

- A short mini-skirt will increase your boyfriend's *interest rate*.

- Never ask a banker for an opinion. They'll rarely give you their two cents worth.

- Save *more* than just your pennies for a rainy day, or you might get soaked.

- Too many trips to the ATM can hurt your IRA.

- A low-fat diet should help curb your *rate of inflation*.

- Nickel and diming your friends will make you worth a mint.

- Always use cash to purchase condoms. No one likes a rubber check.

Steven Spielberg

- Never shout "movie" in a crowded firehouse.

- The key to good movie-making is the ability to go from *real*-to-reel.

- Not brushing your teeth for three days is a good way to produce an unusual *film*.

- Always have breathmints on hand in case of a *Close Encounter* with the opposite sex.

- If you're gonna be out late, *phone home*.

Hillary Clinton

+ Don't assume that a girl who wears a skirt in public doesn't wear the pants at home.

+ One way to tell if you're husband is cheating is if he brings home *Flowers* for no good reason.

+ It's completely inappropriate to perform bondage in the Lincoln bedroom.

+ Never ask a First Lady to play second fiddle.

Donald Trump

- The only habit more expensive than gambling is marriage.

- If your wife is holding all the cards, you'll be the one to ante-up.

- Don't assume your wife is playing Solitaire while you're fooling around with a bunch of *slots*.

- Signing a pre-nuptial agreement is the best way to hedge your bets.

- Always keep your change purse out of reach of a *one-armed bandit*.

Wayne Gretzky

- Don't try to skate through life without any *goals*.

- Watch out for bad guys on the other team. They might try to take your *face-off*.

- Always pay attention to your finances. A bad *check* can wreck your *balance*.

• Always do your best. If you take enough shots, you could end up living like a *King*.

• Gross profits are important, but a good businessman protects his *net*.

70

Billy Joel

◆ Master a musical instrument. You'd be amazed at the gorgeous women you can get if you can play the *Piano, Man*.

◆ Never change for popularity's sake. Your real friends will like you *Just The Way You Are*.

• An elephant's cage is no place for tickling the ivories.

• Having a supermodel lie across the top of your piano will make any man feel like performing.

Kermit the Frog

+ Pay attention. From the gills of tadpoles come words of wisdom.

+ Don't expect many job offers if you have no experience. It's not easy being green.

+ Never invite a pig to a barbecue.

+ Don't waste $50 on a pedicure if you have webbed feet.

- A fresh "Raid No-Pest Strip" can cut down on your weekly grocery bill.

- Look before you leap or you may end up in over your head.

- Just because you're in someone's will, don't wish for them to *croak*.

72

Steven Seagal

- Never tell a martial arts expert to break a leg.

- Stop and think before you tease a guy about his ponytail.

- How you end a relationship says a lot about you. Try not to rip someone's heart out.

- Never give a slap-on-the-wrist when a good ass-kicking would suffice.

- Just because someone is constipated, you don't have to kick the crap out of them.

- A handsome guy who mistakenly turns into a gay bar may soon find himself *Under Seige*.

Neil Armstrong

+ Don't forget to ask your little astronauts if they have to go to the bathroom while you're still on the launching pad.

+ It's not nice to call an oily-skinned teen a "crater-face."

+ Marry someone who has both feet on the ground.

- Shoot for the moon and you may end up eclipsing your wildest dreams.

- Watching a plumber bend over to fix a sink is a great way to see a quarter-*moon*.

Michael Jackson

◆ Never add bleach to your bubble bath.

◆ Never trust a plastic surgeon who uses spackle.

◆ If you don't want your wife to be suspicious, never come home with crayon on your collar.

+ Never invite someone to sleep-over who needs a permission slip.

+ If you're gonna talk the moontalk, you'd better be able to walk the moonwalk.

Rush Limbaugh

- On the weekend, try to plan events the whole *family values*.

- Only a fool would Rush to judgement about a talk-show without having listened to it.

- Unless you have hours to spare, don't ask a disc jockey to *talk radio*.

- Never let a tree-hugger near a cactus.

- You'll only find your rich friends in their mansion if you look in the *right wing*.

Michael Jordan

- *Dunk* your donuts, but never *dribble* your milk.
- Choose a line of work that allows you to *travel*.
- No matter how bad a day you've had, you need to *rebound* the next.
- You don't need a college degree to realize that an M.B.A. doesn't pay like the N.B.A.
- Never fail to *take your shot* for fear of rejection.

Carl Sagan

+ Never tease a chubby astronomer about his love for the *Milky Way*.

+ Coming home to your wife after one too many beers will greatly increase your chances of seeing a flying saucer.

+ Avoid those who think the Earth revolves around them.

♦ The quickest way to get a tall glass of water is to use a *Big Dipper*.

♦ Never trust a Peeping Tom who wants to borrow your telescope to look at the *moon*.

Sylvester Stallone

- Don't be too concerned if your career gets off to a *Rocky* start.

- Don't worry about poor Brigitte *Neilsen ratings* affecting your popularity.

- Never buy an oldies album from a discount record store. You could mistakenly end up with *Sly and the Family Stallone*.

• If you learn how to negotiate a good deal, there may be a pot of gold at the end of the *Rambo*.

• Kids, don't go see *Assassins* without your parent's permission, or you risk getting *killed* when they find out.

Disney CEO
Michael Isner

♦ Find out what you're worth before you settle for a *Mickey Mouse* job.

♦ Putting regular coffee in the decaf pot is a great way to make your employees animated.

♦ A turban and pantaloons is a terrific outfit to dress *Aladdin*.

- Never argue with a dwarf. They tend to be short-tempered.

- Don't drug-test an employee just because they're *Goofy* for a couple of days.

Liz Taylor

- A detox center is the best place to catch a fallen star.

- Don't enter a sixth marriage if you can't make it through the day without wishing you still had your *fifth*.

- Filing for divorce is the best way to go about trying to lose a couple hundred useless pounds.

Rodney King

- ◆ You could end up living like a *King* if you're willing to take a few lumps along the road.

- ◆ Never kick a man when he's down.

- ◆ Always carry a camcorder so you can catch those special unexpected moments.

- ◆ If you try to tackle the *pigs*, you should expect *tenderloins*.

- ◆ Summers in L.A. can be brutal. Be careful not to get *beat by the heat*.

Luciano Pavarotti

- Never leave the opera early. It ain't over 'til the fat *man* sings.

- To be a great opera star, it is best to become as well-rounded as possible.

- Never eat garlic bread before a duet.

- Never sing near a pond. You could end up with a frog in your throat.

- People who sing in the shower are bound to feel *head and shoulders* above those who don't.

- Never let the paparazzi near the Pavarotti.

83

Clint Eastwood

♦ You're wasting your time trying to be a courtroom sketch artist unless you're quick-on-the-draw.

♦ Never chase an outlaw into a patch of poison-ivy. You may develop an itchy trigger-finger.

♦ Tell your parents that you love them . . . Go ahead, make their day.

- Never fire six warning shots.

- Never offer a prostitute a swig from your canteen. You can lead the whores to water, but you can't make them drink.

- If you cut in front of the man who is next up at the urinal, you could find yourself *In The Line of Fire*.

84

Dr. Ruth Westheimer

+ A game of bridge is best when *foreplay*.

+ Too many drinks may make it difficult to get up.

+ Crafts are great to do in your spare time. Find something you *lovemaking*.

- Never grind your own organ.

- The best way to make cappucccino is to turn the heat up slowly... letting the steam rise gently, until the froth peaks... and it *explodes* with flavor!

Garth Brooks

♦ The further you drive from the city lights, the easier it is to spot a country star.

♦ Always accept a party invitation from a nerd. Nothing beats watching a square dance.

♦ Don't give your girlfriend a hickey. Nobody likes to go home with a redneck.

- Even if its on sale, never buy a nine-gallon hat.

- A reputable music store is the best place to do your guitar-*pickin'*.

Bruce Springsteen

+ Unfortunately for term-limit advocates, most politicians are *Born To Run*.

+ Singing the same tune as *The Boss* will make your job much easier.

+ Don't just buy your grandmother a rocking chair — teach her how to *rock!*

+ Take pride in American ingenuity. Most of the great technological innovations of our time were *Born In The U.S.A.*

Boris Yeltsin

- Don't be constantly *Russian* from one place to another.

- An *Iron Curtain* will keep your bathroom floor dry no matter how long you shower.

- When all the trees in your country are dying from radiation, it may be time to *Chernobyl* a new leaf.

- Don't call eveything you disagree with "a load of Bolshevik."

88

Willard Scott

+ Forgetting your wife's birthday could put your sex-life in a deep freeze.

+ You don't have to wait 'til Autumn to turn a new leaf.

+ Look out for salesmen trying to give you a snow job. Some of them really know how to shovel it.

- Never ask someone with false teeth to blow out 100 birthday candles.

- When you're a high-paid weatherman, *every* cloud has a silver lining.

Jacques Cousteau

+ It's never appropriate to fish for a compliment.

+ Don't be the first guy to test that old "punch a shark in the nose" theory.

+ Never swim *down*stream during the salmon's mating season.

+ It's hard to be cocky when you remember that your ancestors were pond scum.

◆ Read invitations carefully. Wearing the wrong outfit to a dinner party will make you feel like a fish out of water.

◆ Never snorkel in your neighbor's jacuzzi.

Madonna

+ Be careful where you point your bra. You could put someone's eye-out.

+ If you know where to draw the *Borderline* with your dates, you can remain *Like A Virgin* for quite some time.

+ Stretch before you perform. It's easier to gyrate your pelvis if you're already extremely loose.

- You'll usually score with a guy if you're not wearing a lot of *Material, Girl.*

- Don't fondle yourself in public. It rubs most people the wrong way.

- Don't fire a good choreographer just for waltzing in late.

George Burns

- Just because someone has *silver* hair and is in their *gold*en years, don't treat them as a commodity.

- Never date a girl who's young enough to be your great-great-great grandaughter.

- If you have dentures, never bite off more than you can chew.

- Save your anti-smoking speech for the young. You'll never change an old fogey with a stogey.

- A fine wine and an old fart both tend to mellow with age.

- If you're a *smooth* talker, women don't mind a few *wrinkles.*

- Don't bother asking a friend with Alzheimers to "stop me if you've heard this one before."

Tom Hanks

- Visit *Philadelphia,* it's full of people with *discriminating* taste.

- The best actors usually make a *Splash* in their debut.

- Sometimes a long talk with a stranger on a park bench can help you see the *Forrest* through the trees.

- Nice guys finish first. No one wants to give an *Oscar* to a *grouch*.

- Don't judge a student entirely based on his S.A.T.'s. After all, stupid is as stupid does.

93

Pope John Paul II

- Don't be a devil-worshipper. You won't have a prayer.

- To be a great leader you must be willing to wear many hats.

- *Abstinence* makes the heart grow fonder.

- Never wear white to an exorcism.

- Finding the shortest route to your church will prevent you from being a *roamin'* Catholic.

- Never tell someone who's having a sneezing fit to count their blessings.

Tonya Harding

- To be the best, sometimes you have to go out there and *break a leg*.

- Never be jealous of another skater's figure.

- If you don't control a hot temper, you'll find yourself skating on thin ice.

- Be wary of those whose laces are strung too tightly.

- Never send a *boy*friend to do a hit*man*'s job.

Olympic Diving Champion
Greg Louganis

+ Never *take the plunge* unless you've fallen *head-over-heels*.

+ Too many beers can make your *belly flop*.

+ Competitive diving can be a real *springboard* to future successes.

+ You can't win a gold medal if you're not willing to *work your way up the ladder*.

+ The great ones don't need to make a *splashy* entrance.

David Hasselhoff

- Don't let your stunt double go swimming until an hour after you've eaten.

- Never offer a glass of water to a drowning man.

- Don't be afraid to hire someone who's a little wet behind the ears.

- Sometimes people won't recognize how good a job you're doing until you make a few *waves*.

- Three guys drinking beer and watching Baywatch quickly become a pair of boobs and an ass.

Siskel and Ebert

- When it comes time to eloquently express your opinion, don't be all *thumbs*.

- A jumbo popcorn is a great way to butter up your date.

- Going to a movie before you read the review can be a *critic*al mistake.

- Never give your fiancee a *Sneak Preview*.

- Unfortunately, the scariest part of most horror movies is the price of the tickets.

- Always give credits where credits are due.

98

Ed McMahon

◆ You can make a career being a second banana even if you don't have *appeal*.

◆ A cloudless night is best for a *Starsearch*.

◆ Buy a copy of this book for a friend, or it might end up at the *Publisher's Clearing House*.

99

Lorena Bobbit

- Leaving an abusive husband permanently is the best way to scar him for life.

- Don't argue with your spouse. You may leave them feeling *detached*.

- For couples who can't get along, it may be best to sever all ties.

- Don't threaten to divorce a woman who says she'll take half of *everything* you have.

100

H & R Block President
Henry Block

• Filing your returns without professional help can be quite *taxing*.

• If you meet the I.R.S. without a C.P.A., you'll be D.O.A.

• Only a *block*head wouldn't take advantage of all the tax loopholes available.

- Never refer to your children as your "little deductions."

- Running a home business can do your *internal revenue* a great service.

Jim Carrey

• Always get a joker to play a *Riddler*.

• Look out for class clowns. They might end up making an *Ace* of themselves.

• Never *Mask* your true personality. Your real friends will accept you no matter how wierd you are.

- As *Dumb* as you may be, a *dumber* friend will always make you look good.

- If you plan on producing a poorly written comedy, you better hire someone who can *Carrey* the movie.

Mafia Kingpin
John Gotti

◆ Don't send an underling to a massage parlor alone. He could end up being *rubbed-out.*

◆ Leaving your wallet in your pants at the dry-cleaners is a good way to get your *money laundered.*

◆ A personal computer is a great tool for keeping your *crime* more *organized.*

- In the mafia, not a *dagos* by without being reminded that you're an Italian.

- A mobster who makes waves usually ends up on the ocean floor.

Dear Abby
Abigail Van Buren

• When you ask for free advice, you usually get what you pay for.

• Never write an anonymous letter on personalized stationery.

• Even if your washing machine is broken, never air your dirty laundry in public.

• Don't go through life expecting other people to solve your problems.

• If you need to write a letter questioning your boyfriend's behavior, you probably already know what the answer is.

Carl Lewis

- You'll never be a winner if you're always following in another man's footsteps.

- Whenever you hear a pistol, always run for your life.

- The most successful people learn how to take life's hurdles in stride.

- Don't join the track team if you don't want to be judged solely on your race.

- When it comes to raising children, don't expect to *ever* see a finish line.

- To be a wealthy track star, you must learn how to give people a *run for their money*.

Lee Iacocca

- If the salesman is giving you the squeeze, chances are he's selling you a lemon.

- When your date asks you for a test-drive, it's a good time to put on the brakes.

- Three square meals a day will prevent you from running out of gas.

- Never buy a K-car without an A-Z warranty.

- You can always count on an *airbag* to expand whenever you run into them.

- Don't be such a perfectionist. Buy American-made cars!

106

Hugh Hefner

- Don't put a woman on a pedestal just to look up her dress.

- Always supply your bunny with plenty of *carats*.

- No matter how long a photo session takes, the best models know how to grin and *bare* it.

◆ Live for today. If your sights are constantly on January, you may *Miss December*.

◆ Never deny a faithful husband his playmates.

Norman Shwarzkopf

- Always be specific. Some people are too damn *General*.

- Around the holidays we all fight the Battle of the Bulge.

- If you listen to a burning *Bush* you may end up in the middle of the desert.

- Bringing home a bad report card is usually called a D-Day.

- Do what you love even if your career is *bombing*.

- Never have a battle of wits with someone who is unarmed.

108

O.J. Simpson

- Never hold a grudge. Be willing to bury the hatchet.

- If you organize your schedule, sometimes you can kill two birds with one stone.

- Don't leave a mess for someone else to clean up.

- Don't take someone's head off just because you disagree with them.

- If the glove fits, hide it.

TITTLES BY CCC PUBLICATIONS

Retail $4.99
"?"
POSITIVELY PREGNANT
SIGNS YOUR SEX LIFE IS DEAD
WHY MEN DON'T HAVE A CLUE
40 AND HOLDING YOUR OWN
CAN SEX IMPROVE YOUR GOLF?
THE COMPLETE BOOGER BOOK
THINGS YOU CAN DO WITH A USELESS MAN
FLYING FUNNIES
MARITAL BLISS & OXYMORONS
THE VERY VERY SEXY ADULT DOT-TO-DOT BOOK
THE DEFINITIVE FART BOOK
THE COMPLETE WIMP'S GUIDE TO SEX
THE CAT OWNER'S SHAPE UP MANUAL
PMS CRAZED: TOUCH ME AND I'LL KILL YOU!
RETIRED: LET THE GAMES BEGIN
MALE BASHING: WOMEN'S FAVORITE PASTIME
THE OFFICE FROM HELL
FOOD & SEX
FITNESS FANATICS
YOUNGER MEN ARE BETTER THAN RETIN-A
BUT OSSIFER, IT'S NOT MY FAULT

Retail $4.95
1001 WAYS TO PROCRASTINATE
THE WORLD'S GREATEST PUT-DOWN LINES
HORMONES FROM HELL II
SHARING THE ROAD WITH IDIOTS
THE GREATEST ANSWERING MACHINE MESSAGES
  OF ALL TIME
WHAT DO WE DO NOW?? (A Guide For New Parents)
HOW TO TALK YOU WAY OUT OF A TRAFFIC TICKET
THE BOTTOM HALF (How To Spot Incompetent
  Professionals)
LIFE'S MOST EMBARRASSING MOMENTS
HOW TO ENTERTAIN PEOPLE YOU HATE
YOUR GUIDE TO CORPORATE SURVIVAL
THE SUPERIOR PERSON'S GUIDE TO EVERYDAY
  IRRITATIONS
GIFTING RIGHT

Retail $3.95
YOU KNOW YOU'RE AN OLD FART WHEN...
NO HANG-UPS
NO HANG-UPS II
NO HANG-UPS III
HOW TO SUCCEED IN SINGLES BARS
HOW TO GET EVEN WITH YOUR EXES
TOTALLY OUTRAGEOUS BUMPER-SNICKERS ($2.95)

Retail $5.95
LITTLE INSTRUCTION BOOK OF THE RICH & FAMOUS
GETTING EVEN WITH THE ANSWERING MACHINE
ARE YOU A SPORTS NUT?
MEN ARE PIGS / WOMEN ARE BITCHES
50 WAYS TO HUSTLE YOUR FRIENDS ($5.99)
HORMONES FROM HELL
HUSBANDS FROM HELL
KILLER BRAS & Other Hazards Of The 50's
IT'S BETTER TO BE OVER THE HILL THAN UNDER IT
HOW TO REALLY PARTY!!!
WORK SUCKS!
THE PEOPLE WATCHER'S FIRLD GUIDE
THE UNOFFICIAL WOMEN'S DIVORCE GUIDE
THE ABSOLUTE LAST CHANCE DIET BOOK

FOR MEN ONLY (How To Survive Marriage)
THE UGLY TRUTH ABOUT MEN
NEVER A DULL CARD
RED HOT MONOGAMY
  (In Just 60 Seconds A Day) ($6.95)

NO HANG-UPS – CASSETTES Retail $4.98

Vol. I:	GENERAL MESSAGES (Female)
Vol. I:	GENERAL MESSAGES (Male)
Vol. II:	BUSINESS MESSAGES (Female)
Vol. II:	BUSINESS MESSAGES (Male)
Vol. III:	'R' RATED MESSAGES (Female)
Vol. III:	'R' RATED MESSAGES (Male)
Vol. IV:	SOUND EFFECTS ONLY
Vol. V:	CELEBRI-TEASE